SQUARE DANCING
is for me

SQUARE DANCING is for me

Mildred Hammond

photographs by
James C. Tabb

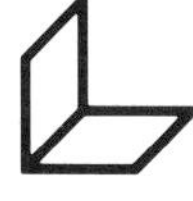

Lerner Publications Company Minneapolis

The author wishes to thank the Dancin' Nomads and their caller, Joe Swartz; the Blue Ridge Twirlers and their caller, Curley Custer; and the parents of the dancers. Special thanks to Roberta Sharp and her assistants, Peggy Smith and Forrest Hammond, teachers of the Mountain State Square Dancers.

Cover photo and photo on page 5 by Jack DeHaven.

To Forrest, Robbie Jo, Judy, David, and Diana

LIBRARY OF CONGRESS CATALOGING IN PUBLICATION DATA

Hammond, Mildred.
Square dancing is for me.

(A Sports for me book)
Summary: Michelle and Andrew join a square dancing club after taking square dancing lessons and learning such steps as the do-sa-do, the see saw, the promenade, and the allemande.
1. Square dancing—Juvenile literature. [1. Square dancing] I. Tabb, James C., ill. II. Title.
III. Series: Sports for me books.
GV1783.H26 1983 793.3′4 82-17134
ISBN 0-8225-1138-X (lib bdg.)

Manufactured in the United States of America

International Standard Book Number: 0-8225-1138-X
Library of Congress Catalog Card Number: 82-17134

1 2 3 4 5 6 7 8 9 10 91 90 89 88 87 86 85 84 83

Hi! I'm Michelle, and this is my cousin Andrew. We're dressed for square dancing. Andrew and I belong to a group called the Mountain State Square Dancers. Everyone in the group loves to square dance. We hope that this book will get you excited about square dancing, too.

Andrew and I first learned about square dancing from our grandparents. Last summer they invited us to go camping with them. On Saturday night at the campgrounds, everyone met at the recreation hall. My grandparents and many of the other campers started to square dance. Andrew and I just watched. It looked like the dancers were having so much fun!

Before long, the dancers asked the newcomers to join in. Andrew and I weren't sure we could follow the steps. But the more experienced dancers helped us, and soon we were dancing along. There were other beginners there that night, so we didn't feel silly when we made mistakes.

When Andrew and I returned home from the camping trip, we joined a square dance class for children. Our teacher was Ms. Sharp. She told us that square dancing is done by groups of eight people—pairs of four boys and four girls. The dancers take their starting positions in a **squared set**, which is an imaginary square on the floor. Each pair of dancers stands on one side of the square, facing the center. This square formation is what gives square dancing its name.

We learned that the dancers who have their backs to the music are couple number one. They are called the **head couple** and are in **Position 1**. The dancers across the square from them in **Position 3** are also a **head couple**. They are couple number 3. The dancers in **Position 2** and **Position 4** are called **side couples**, or couple number 2 and couple number 4.

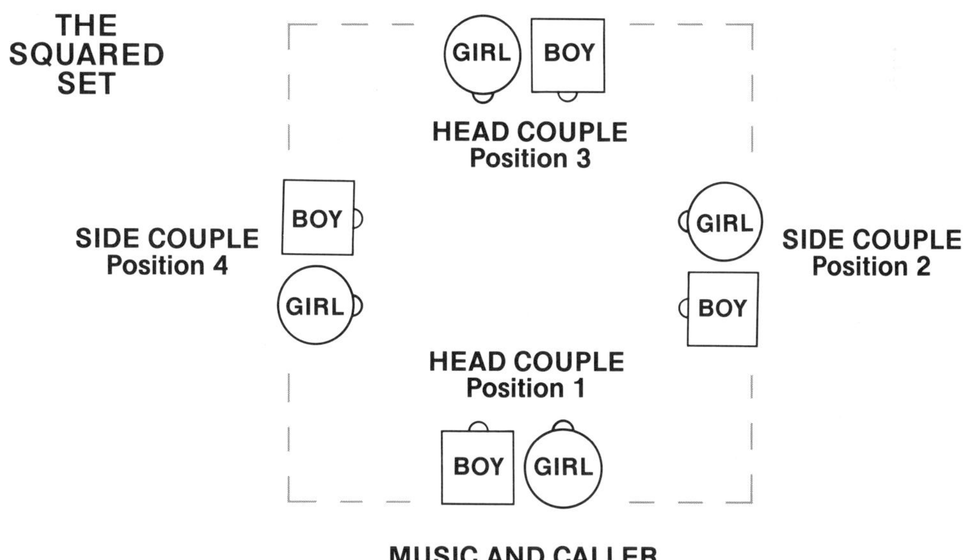

When dancers **square up**, they stand in their starting positions in the set. We learned to keep our set small so that we'd have time to do all the steps. To find the right size for your set, hold your arms outstretched. The side couples and head couples should touch fingertips at the corners of the square.

The eight dancers in a set move to the directions of a **caller**. The caller calls out the steps he or she wants the dancers to do. Our class didn't have a **live caller** like the one at the campgrounds. Instead we followed calls that had been recorded on cassette tapes. Ms. Sharp said that we would learn many calls and would soon know them by heart.

The caller may ask you to **honor your partner**. If you are a boy, your partner is the girl on your right. If you are a girl, your partner is the boy on your left. Andrew was my partner. We turned to face each other. Then Andrew bowed from the waist, holding his right hand across his stomach and his left hand behind him. I was wearing pants, so I just pretended to hold my skirt out as I curtsied.

You may hear the call to **honor your corner**. A boy's corner is the girl on his left. A girl's corner is the boy on her right. To honor your corner, turn to face your corner and then bow or curtsey.

When the caller says to **circle to the left** or **circle to the right**, we all join hands and move around in a circle. Ms. Sharp showed us the correct way to hold our hands as we circled. The boys hold their palms up, and the girls rest their hands in them, palms down. To help keep the circle small and round, try to keep both arms bent at the same angle.

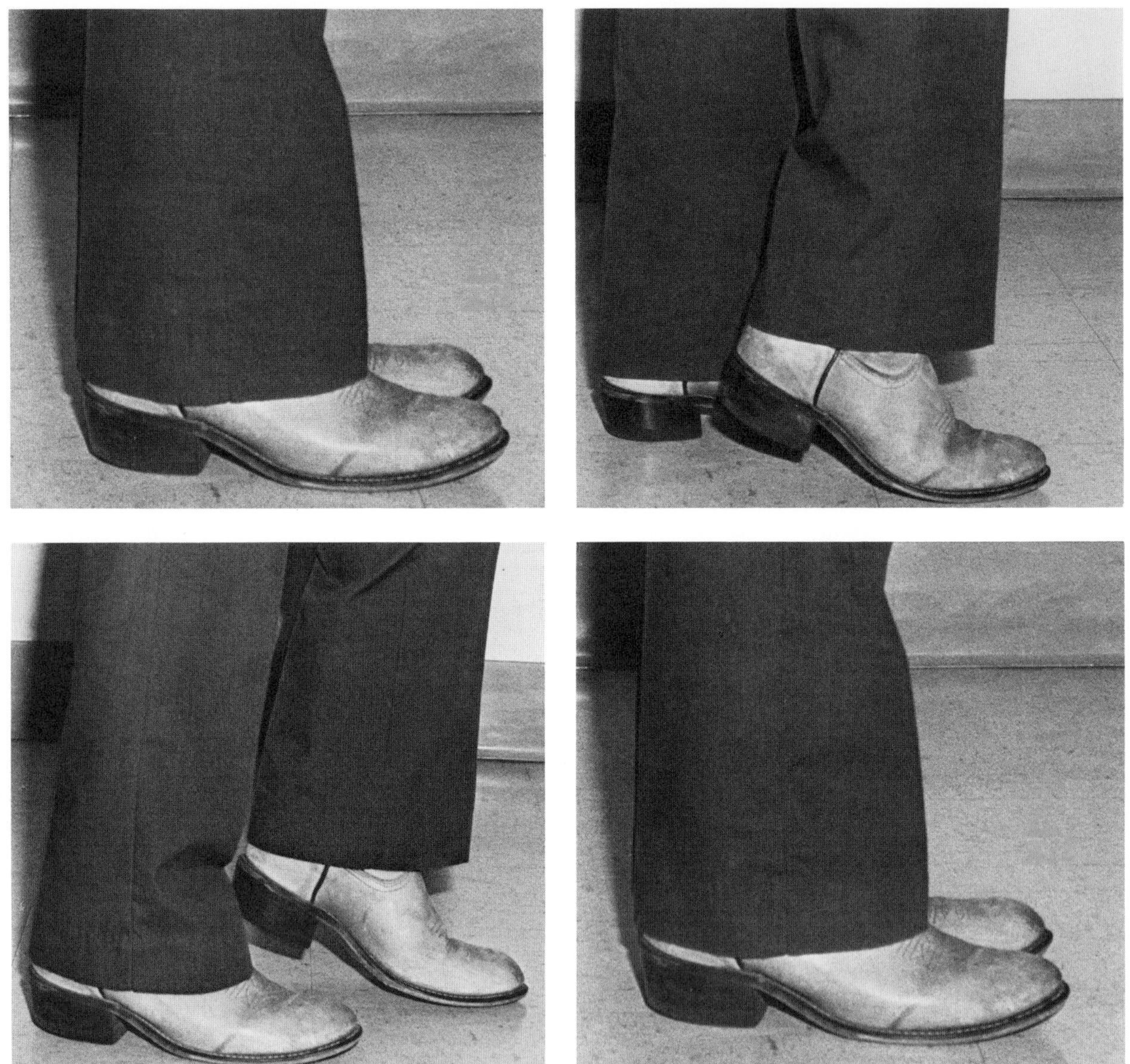

As we circle, we turn our bodies so that we can walk forward. We learned to walk with a **shuffle step**. The shuffle step is more comfortable and less tiring than normal walking. To do the shuffle step, lift your heels and slide forward on the balls of your feet. This is a toe-to-heel motion rather than the heel-to-toe motion you usually do when you walk.

We also learned that **timing** is very important. Timing is matching your steps to the beat of the music. The caller knows how many beats of music to allow for each call. If your timing is off, you may not be in position to start the next call.

Another important call is the **do-sa-do**. You begin this call standing face to face with your partner. Next you walk forward past your partner's right shoulder.

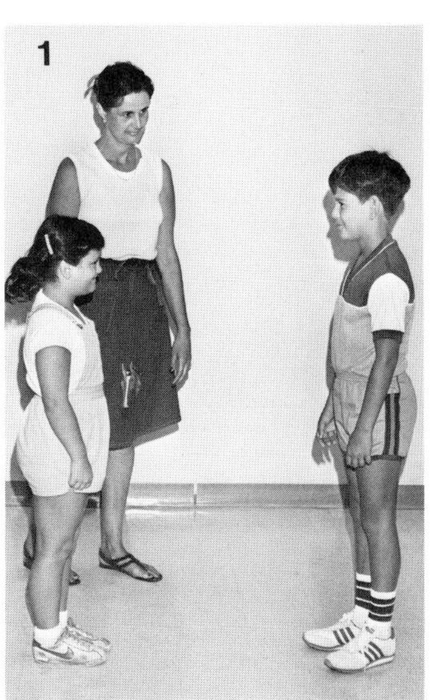
1

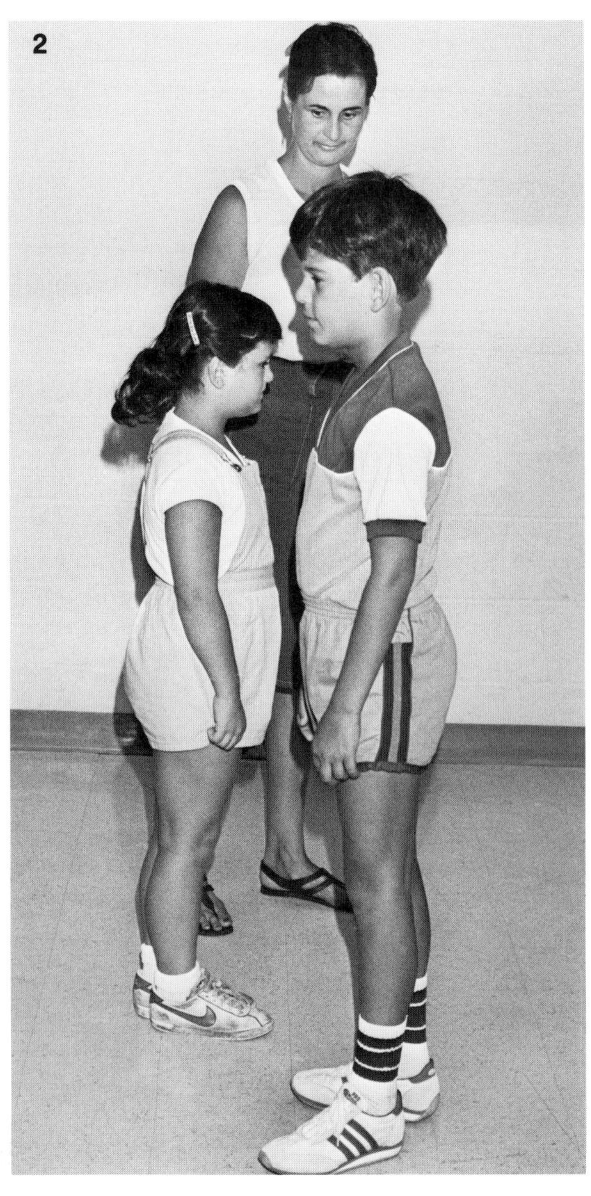
2

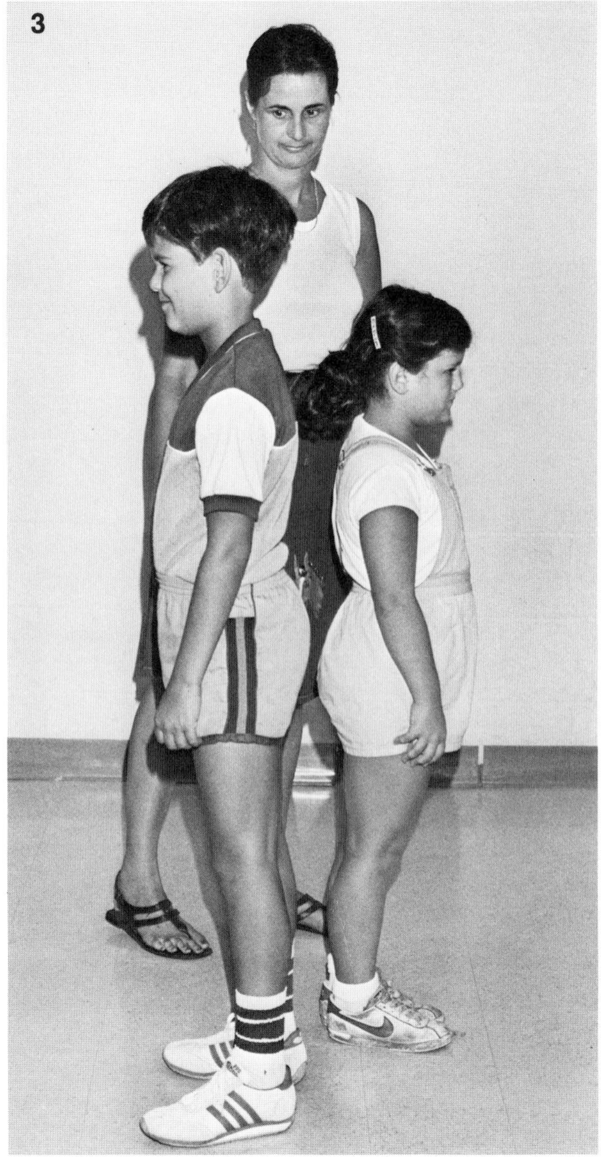
3

Once you are past your partner, step to the right and walk backwards past your partner's left shoulder. You'll end up facing each other again.

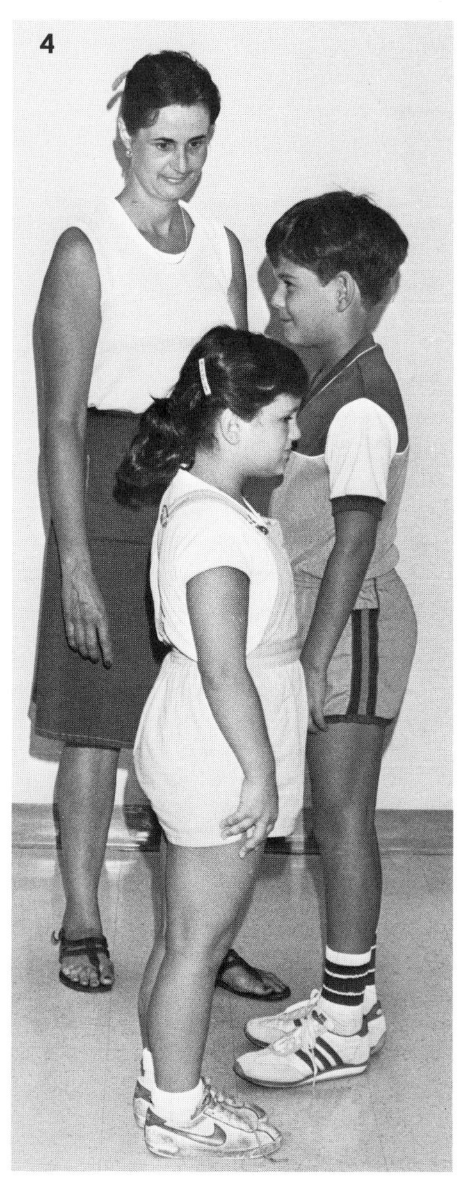

4

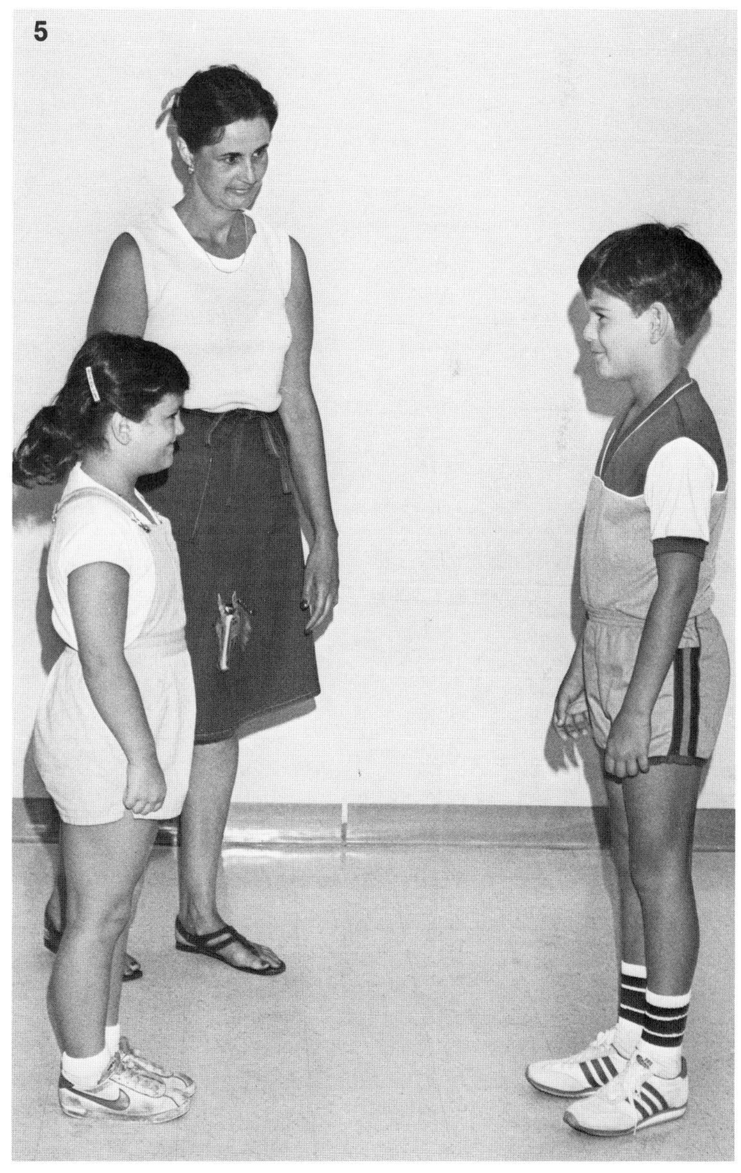

5

The **see saw** is very much like the do-sa-do. To start the see saw, you face your partner. Then you walk forward passing *left* shoulders.

1

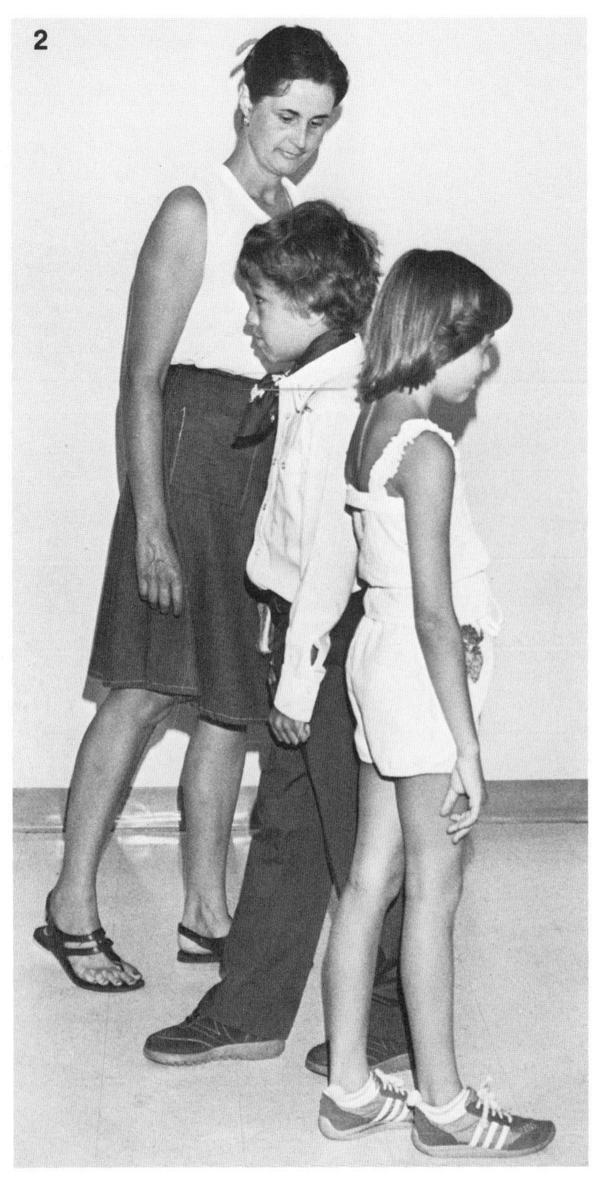
2

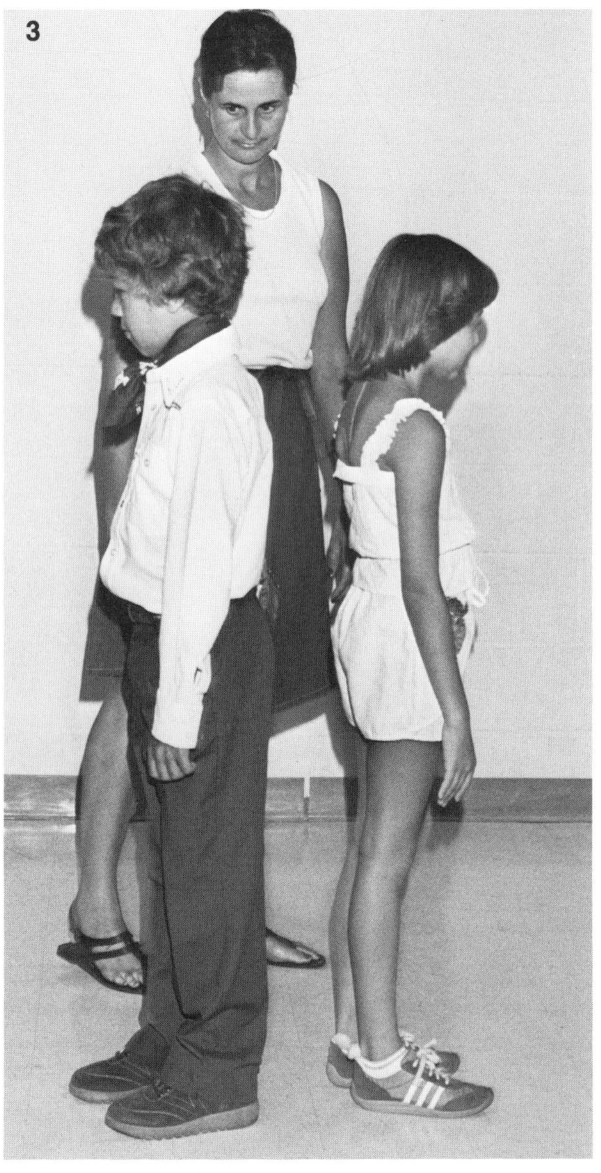
3

On the return to your starting position, you step backward past your partner's *right* shoulder. Keep facing each other until you hear the next call.

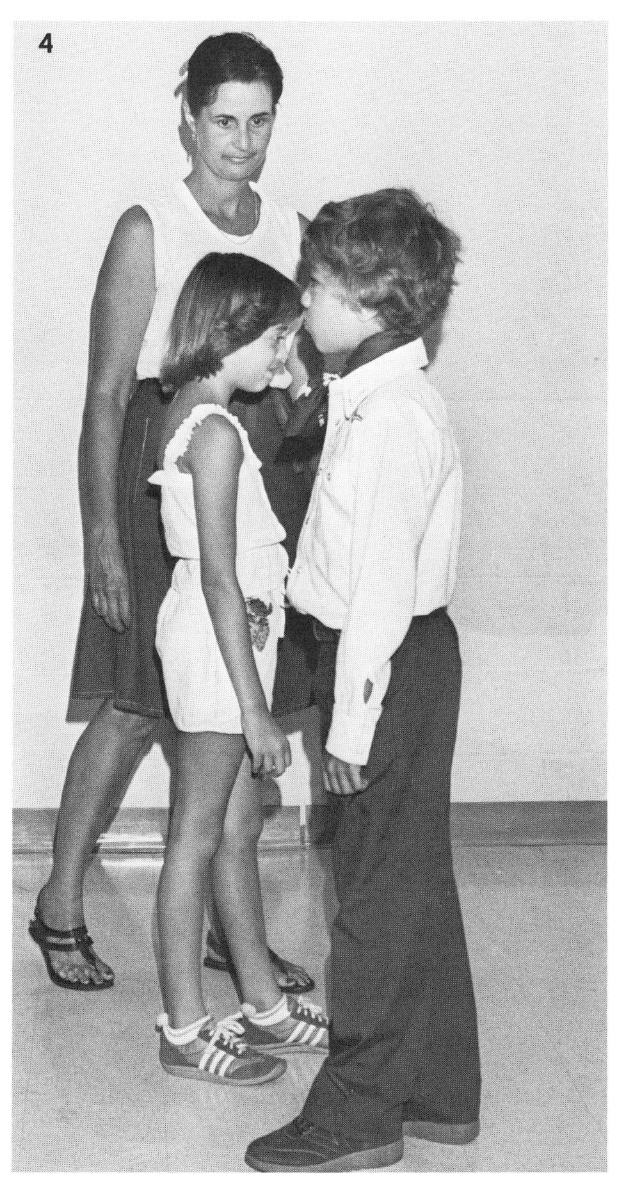

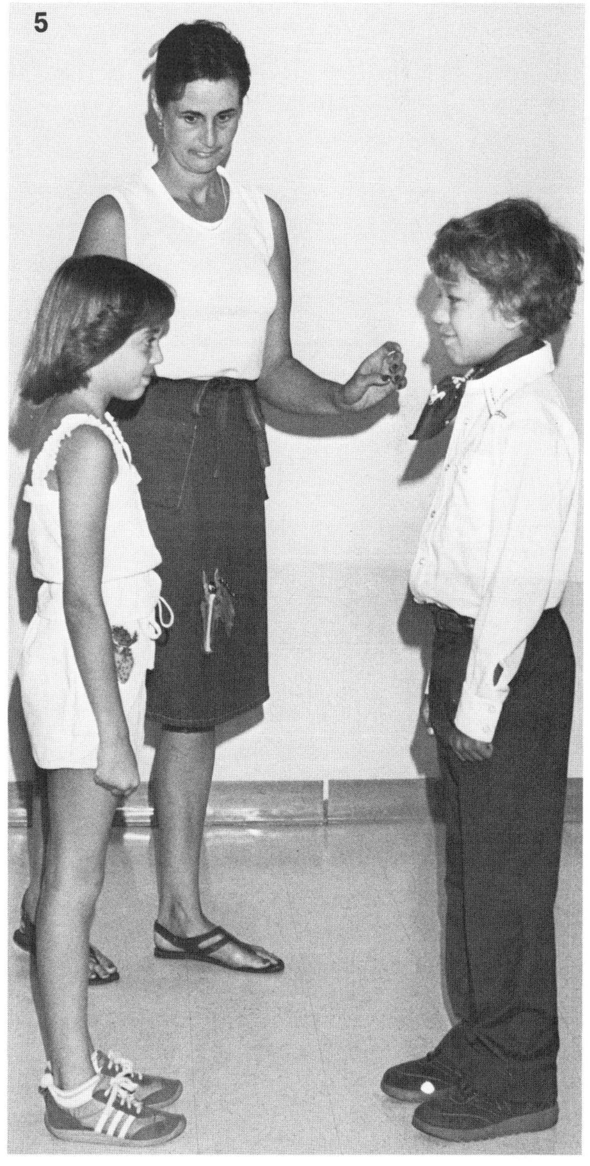

Our class learned new calls each week, and Ms. Sharp had us practice them one after another. She mixed calls into interesting patterns. Because there are so many different ways to combine calls, every dance can be a new one. We quickly discovered that if we didn't listen to the calls carefully, we would make mistakes.

If you make a mistake, return to your **home position.** That is your starting position in the set. As soon as you hear a call that you can do, you can begin to dance again.

Because it is so important for everyone to hear the calls and the music, you should not talk or clap during a dance. You can clap and cheer at the end of the dance. Our class always says a special thank you to the other dancers at the end of each dance. We extend our hands and hold them together in the center of our set. Then we all say "thank you" as we pull our hands back.

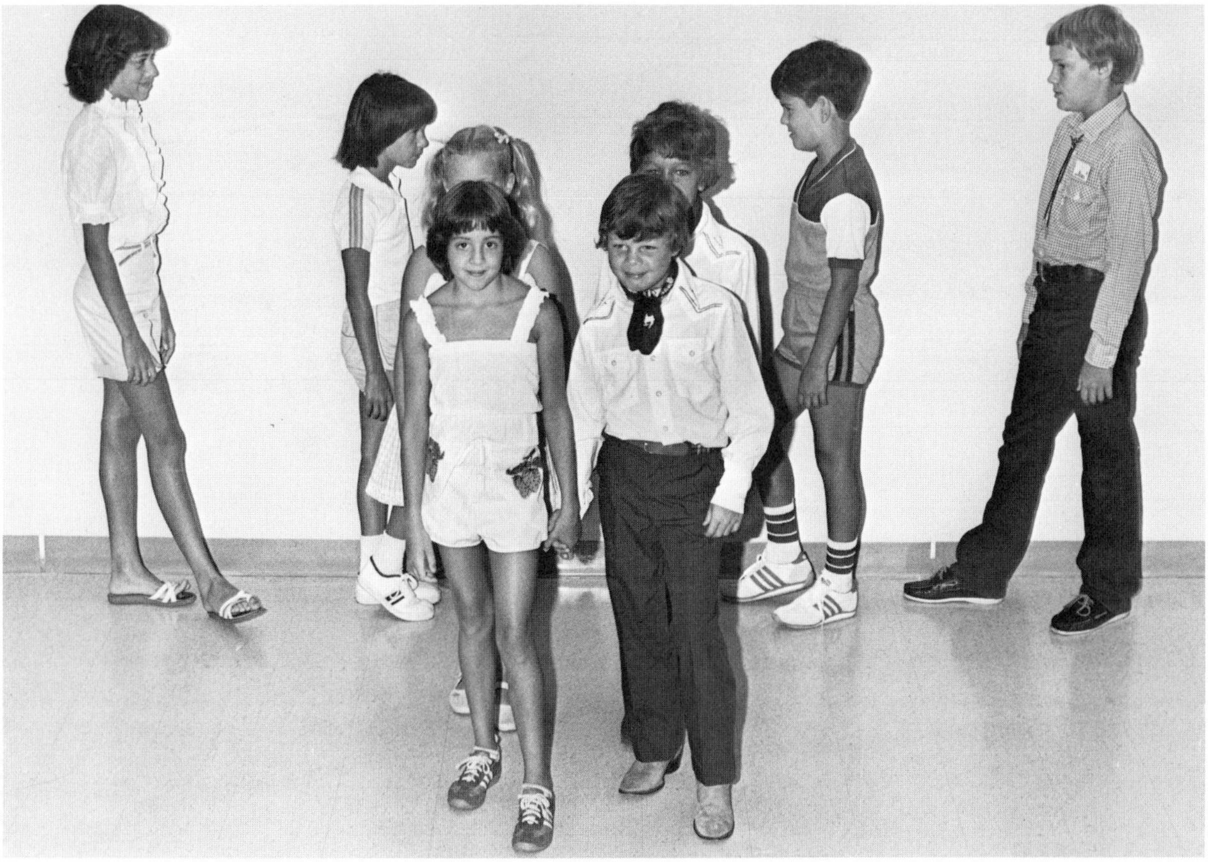

Our class had several methods for finding new partners. One way was a number system. Girls and boys wore tags with numbers on them. Those wearing matching numbers were partners.

Sometimes we lined up by height. The boys formed one line, and the girls formed another. When the two lines met, we had new partners.

Ms. Sharp said that it is good to mix with everyone. You can learn from those who dance better than you. And you can also learn by helping those who are a little slower.

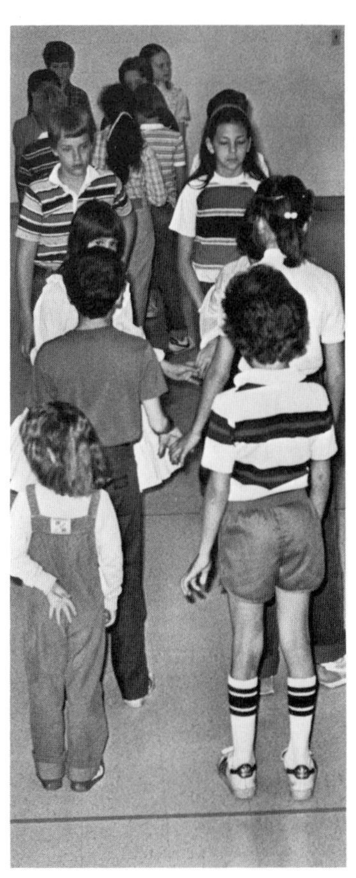

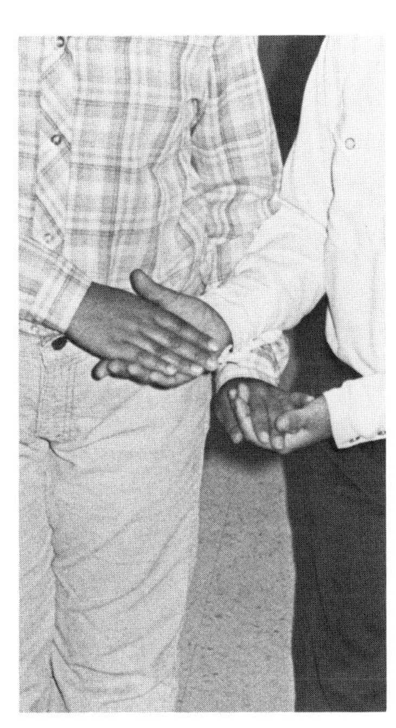

As our classes continued, we would **workshop**, or learn new calls. One call, the **promenade**, is a walk around the circle, with boys on the inside and girls on the outside. The boys promenade with their partner to their home position. At the end of the promenade, you turn to face the center of the set. Partners hold hands in the skating position, with right hands together and left hands clasped below them.

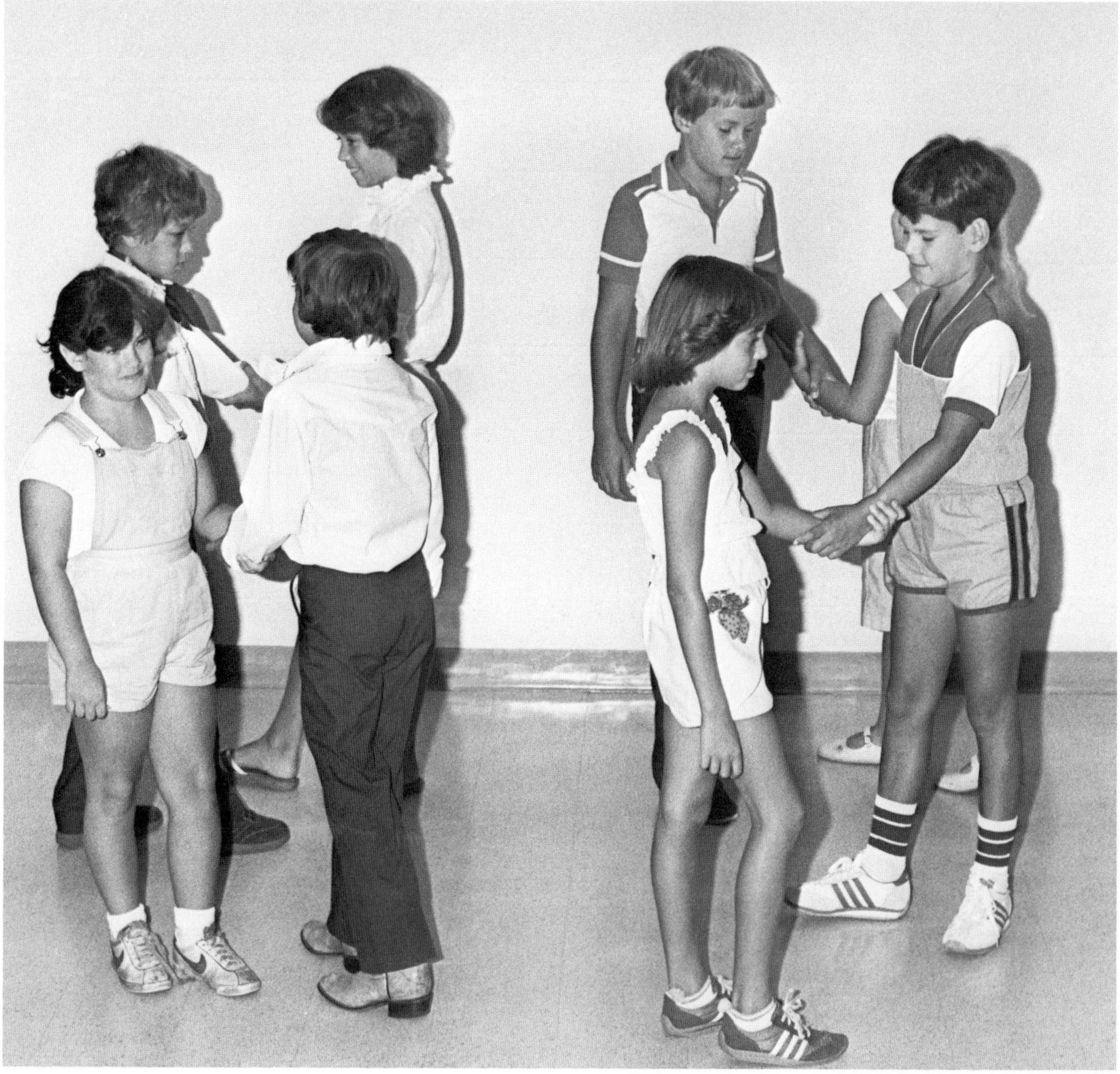

An **allemande left** is performed with your corner. To do this call, step forward and grasp your corner's left forearm with your left hand. Keep walking forward in a half circle until you are in your corner's starting position.

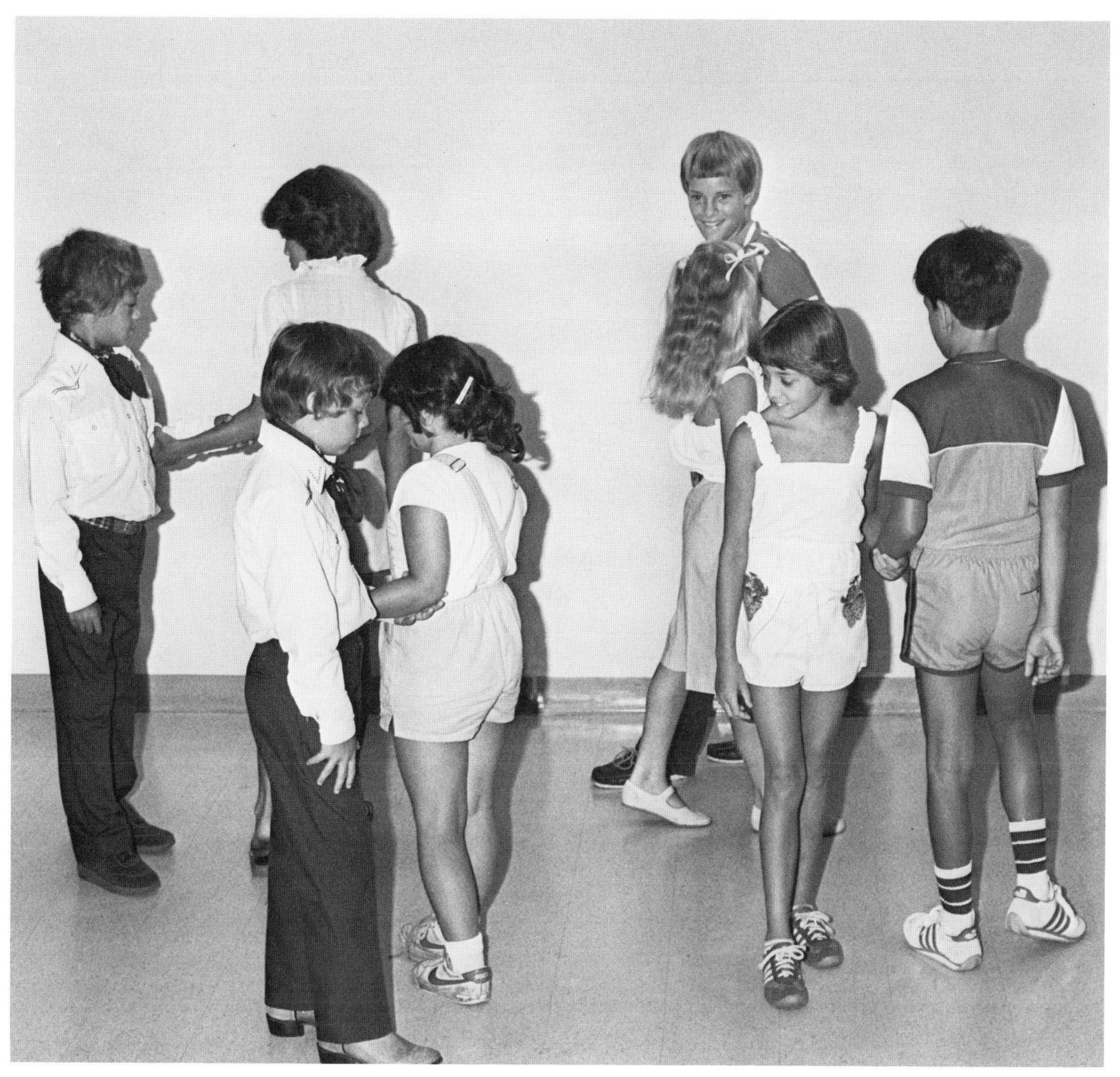

Now gently pull with your left arm and move forward past your corner's left shoulder. Drop hands and end facing your partner.

The **right and left grand** is often the call following an allemande left. This is a movement around the circle. Partners face each other at the start of a right and left grand. To do the call, give your partner your right hand as if you were going to shake hands. Then gently pull forward past your partner, drop your right hand, and extend your left hand to the next dancer in line. Pull by each dancer using your right hand, then left hand, until you meet your partner again.

Partners can turn in place by doing the **courtesy turn**. To do this call, the partners hold left hands. The boy's right hand is put in the girl's right hand, which is held palm out at the small of her back. The partners turn in place as the girl walks forward and the boy steps backward.

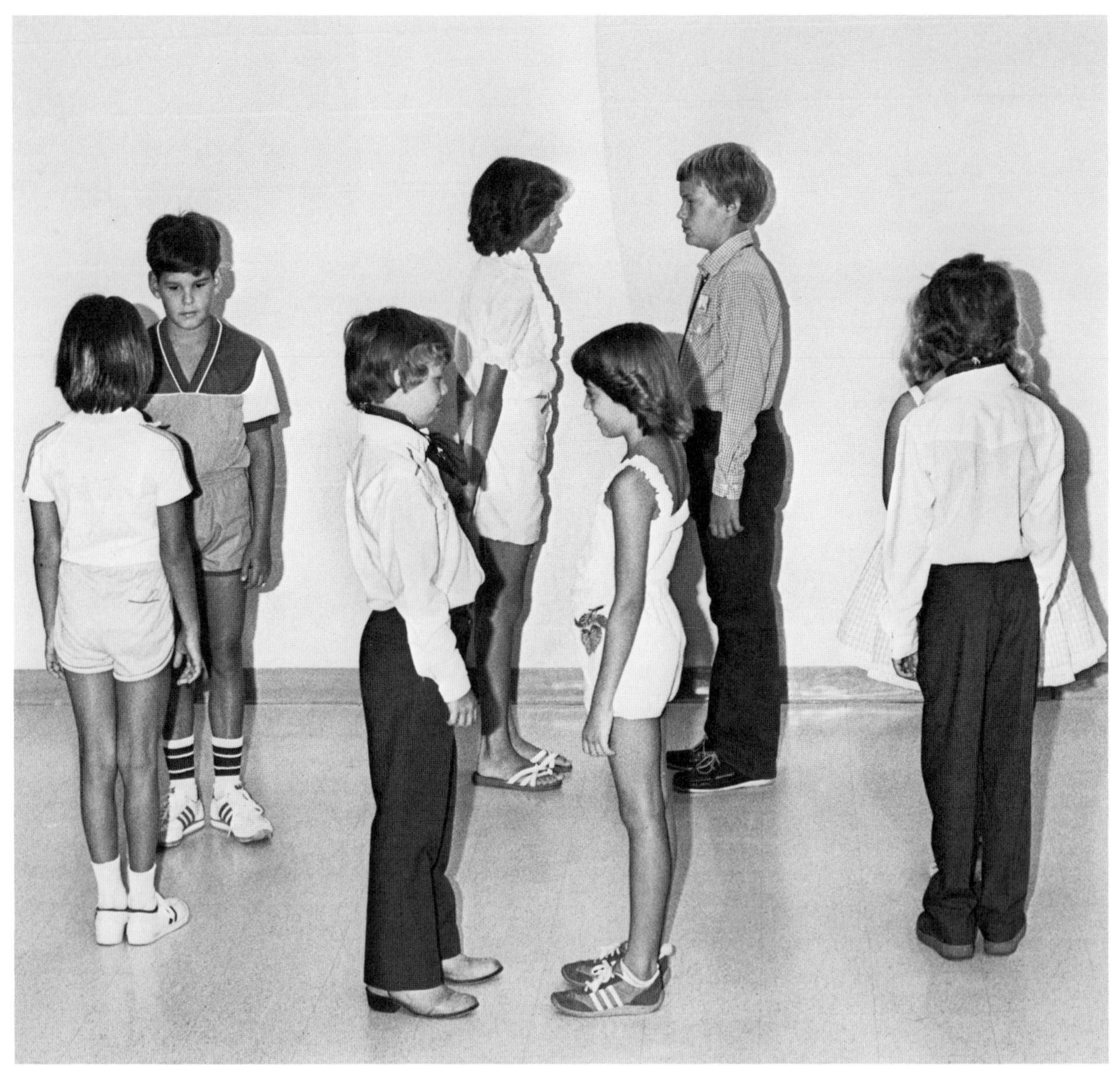

Some calls are very easy to learn because they're very much like another call. **Weave the ring,** for example, is a right and left grand done without using the hands.

To weave the ring, keep your circle small as you weave in and out. Stop when you meet your partner. Boys move in one direction and girls in the other around the circle.

The **right hand star** is another beautiful formation. Girls hold their right hands, palms together, in the center of the set. Then they move around in a circle. When boys do the right hand star, they grasp wrists as they circle around.

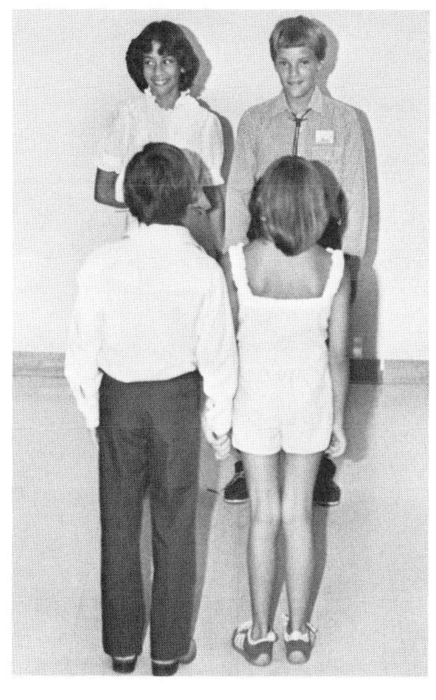

The **pass thru** can be called when dancers are facing each other. As you walk forward, you pass the facing dancer's right shoulder. You will be facing out of the square. Listen for the next call.

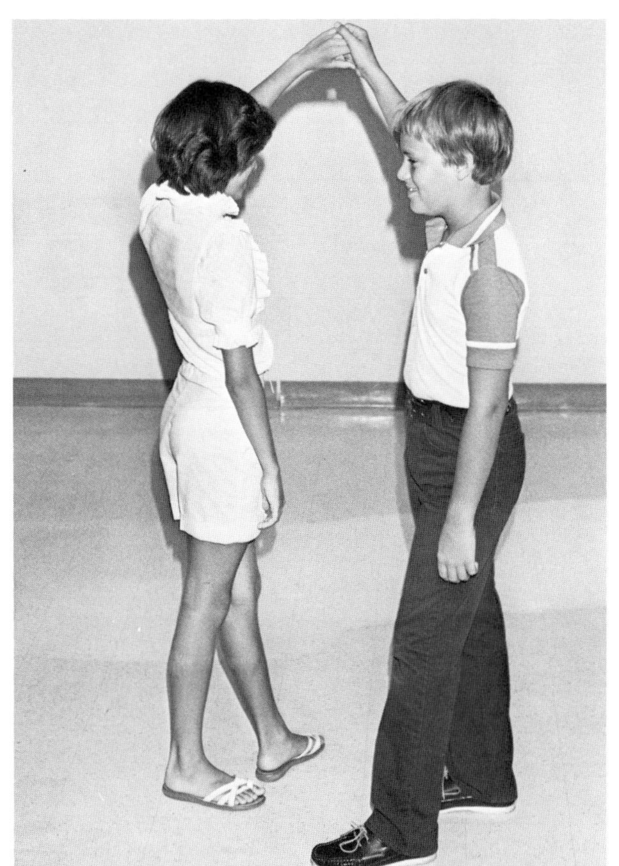
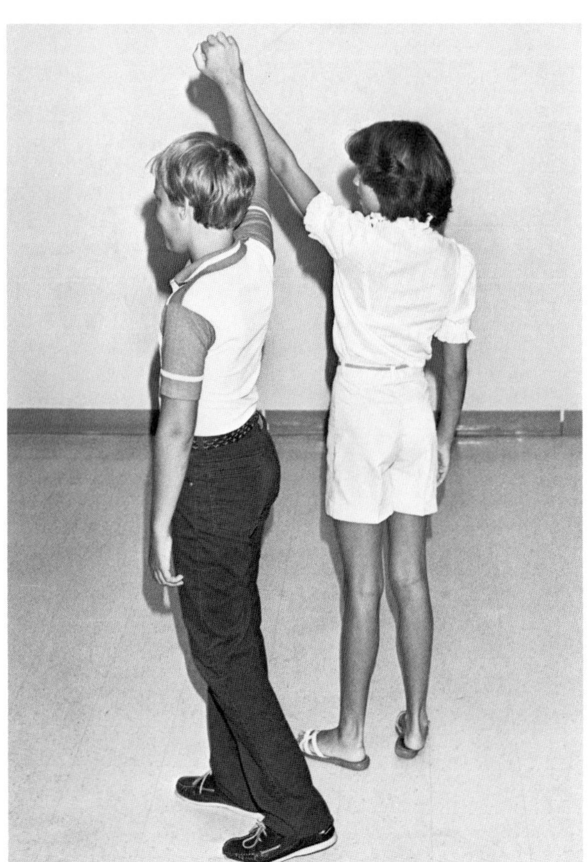
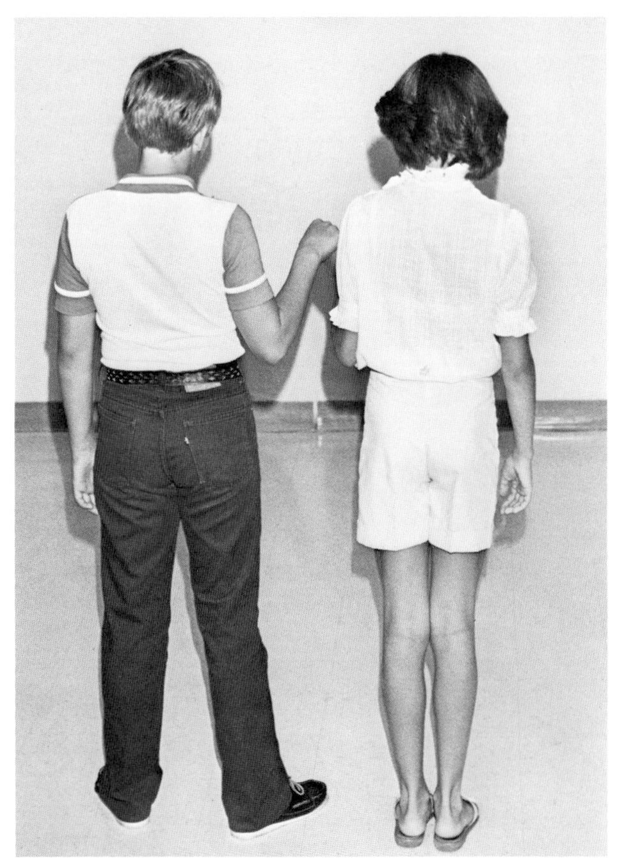

The **California twirl** is a way to exchange places with your partner and to change the direction you and your partner are facing. The girl starts at the boy's right side. The boy takes her left hand in his right hand, and they raise them in an arch. The girl then walks forward under the arch, and the boy walks forward into her starting position.

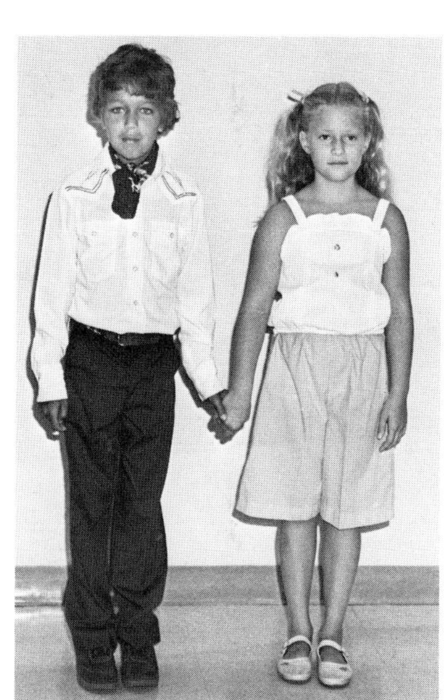

Another way to exchange places is the **rollaway half sashay.** First the partners join hands. Then the dancer on the right, usually the girl, steps forward and rolls across in front of her partner. He sidesteps to the right to exchange places.

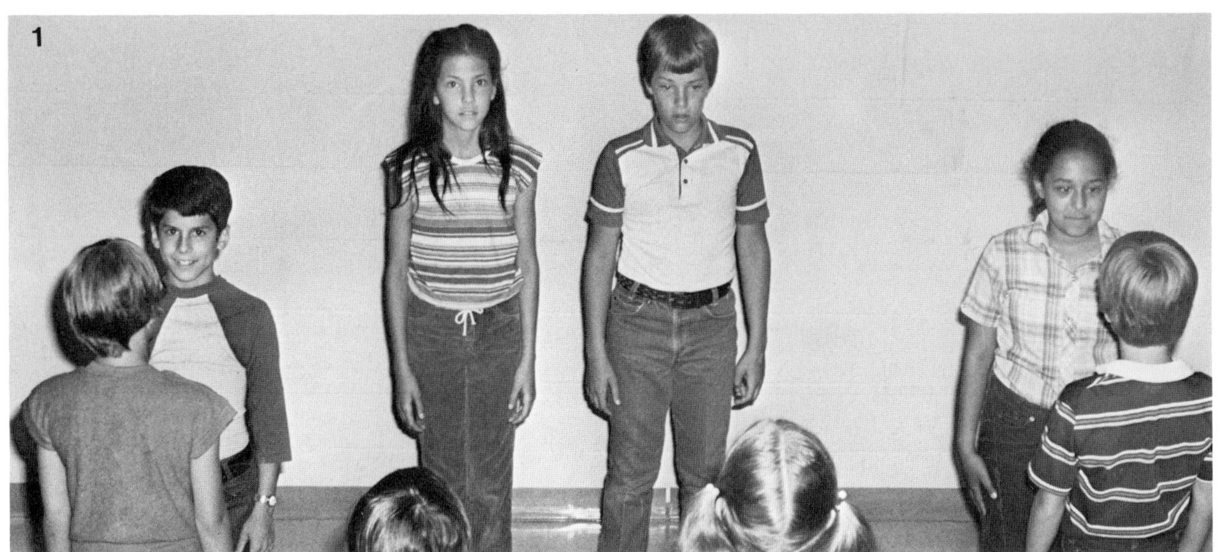
1

2

3

The opening call for one of my favorite dances is "**Sides face! Grand square!**" The grand square is a continuous movement of all dancers within the square. The sides move in one pattern and the heads in another. Each dancer walks a small square within the larger square. These are the steps for the grand square:

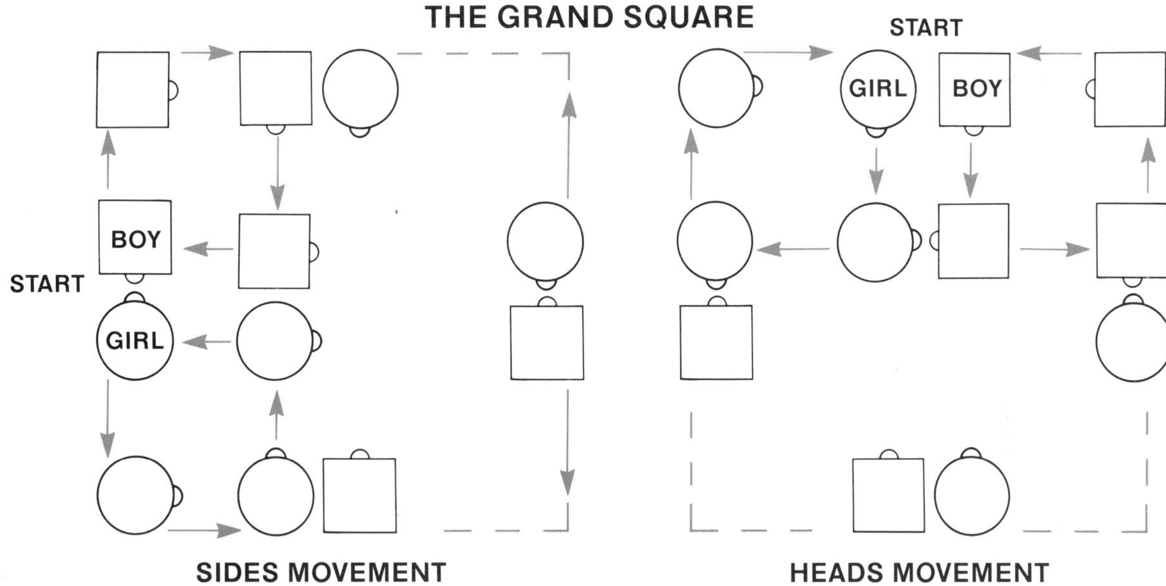

1. **Sides:** Face your partner, walk backwards counting one, two, three, and then turn to face into the square. **Heads:** Move forward into the square. Count to three as you move, and turn on the fourth step.

2. **Sides:** Walk forward, count one, two, three, and turn as you move into the head position. **Heads:** You will be facing your partner. Back away to the side position and turn on step four.

3. **Sides:** Move forward into the square. Count to three again, and turn on the fourth step. **Heads:** Back away to the corner of the square, count to three, and turn to face your partner.

4. **Sides:** Back away to the side position. Do not turn. **Heads:** Walk toward your partner. Count one, two, three, four. Do not turn.

5. **Sides:** Reverse your steps, again count to three, and turn until you are in your starting position. **Heads:** You are in home position facing your partner. Do not turn. Reverse your steps. When you have completed the count, you will be with your partner in your starting position.

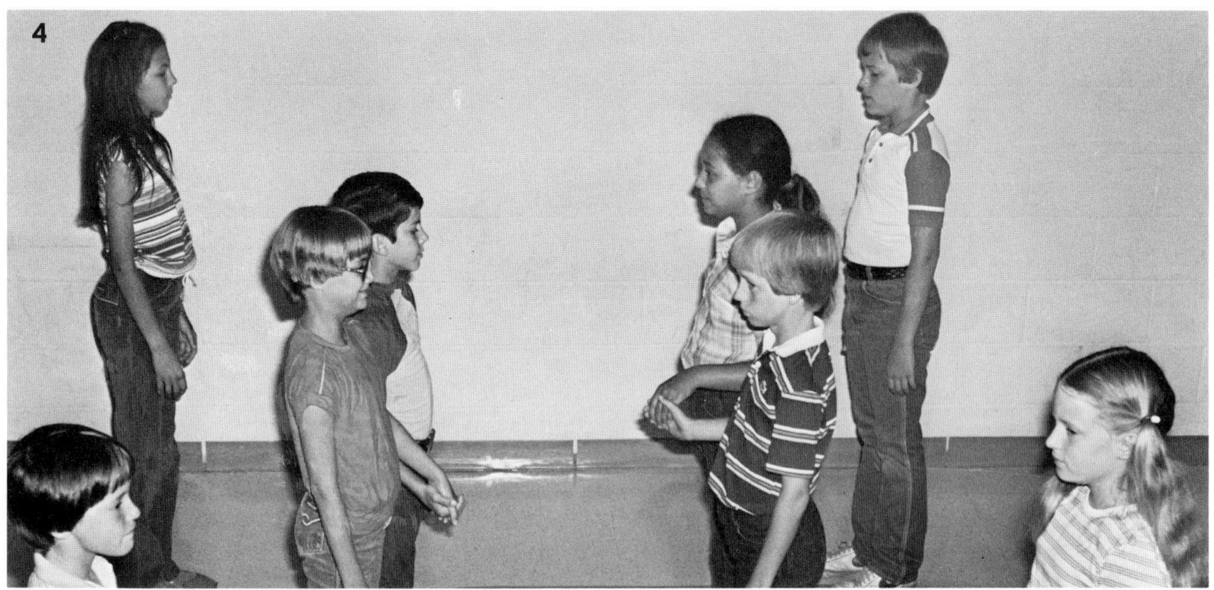

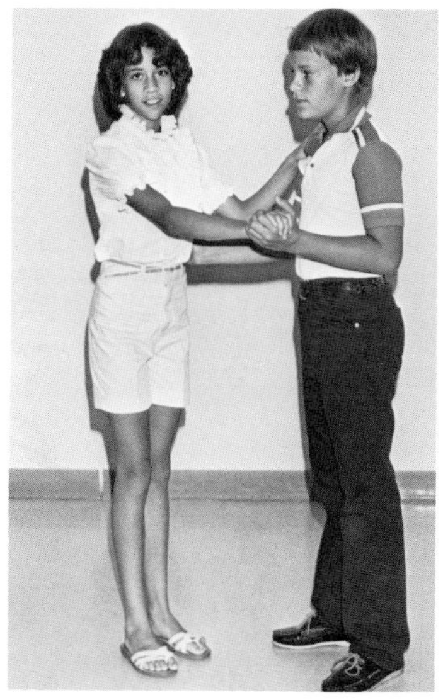

Swing your partner! For this call, each step of the swing movement is on the beat of the music. It is a basic dance step and is smooth and pretty. The boy's left arm, bent at the elbow, will hold the right hand of the girl. The boy's right hand is at the girl's waist. The girl will place her left arm on the boy's right shoulder. Use short walking or shuffling steps while turning around.

When our square dance classes ended, Andrew and I and most of the class decided we wanted to continue dancing. We named our group the Mountain State Squares. It was fun getting together with friends who liked square dancing as much as we did. We especially had fun choosing our outfits. I really love the full petticoats the girls wear!

One of the first things our group did was to attend an adult square dancing **exhibition,** or show. These dancers were at a higher level of square dancing. They knew the more difficult calls and danced with ease and energy.

Some of the dancers had just returned from the National Square Dance Convention. They were still excited about the trip. There are 6 million square dancers across the country. Over 39,000 had attended the National Convention! With over 300 live callers, the dancers could dance from the basic level to the most difficult levels.

One of the nicest things about square dancing is sharing. We invite other groups to dance with us, and other groups ask us to dance with them. The Mountain State Squares have been invited to dance at our school's spring banquet. We are also going to dance at the park for the Fourth of July celebration.

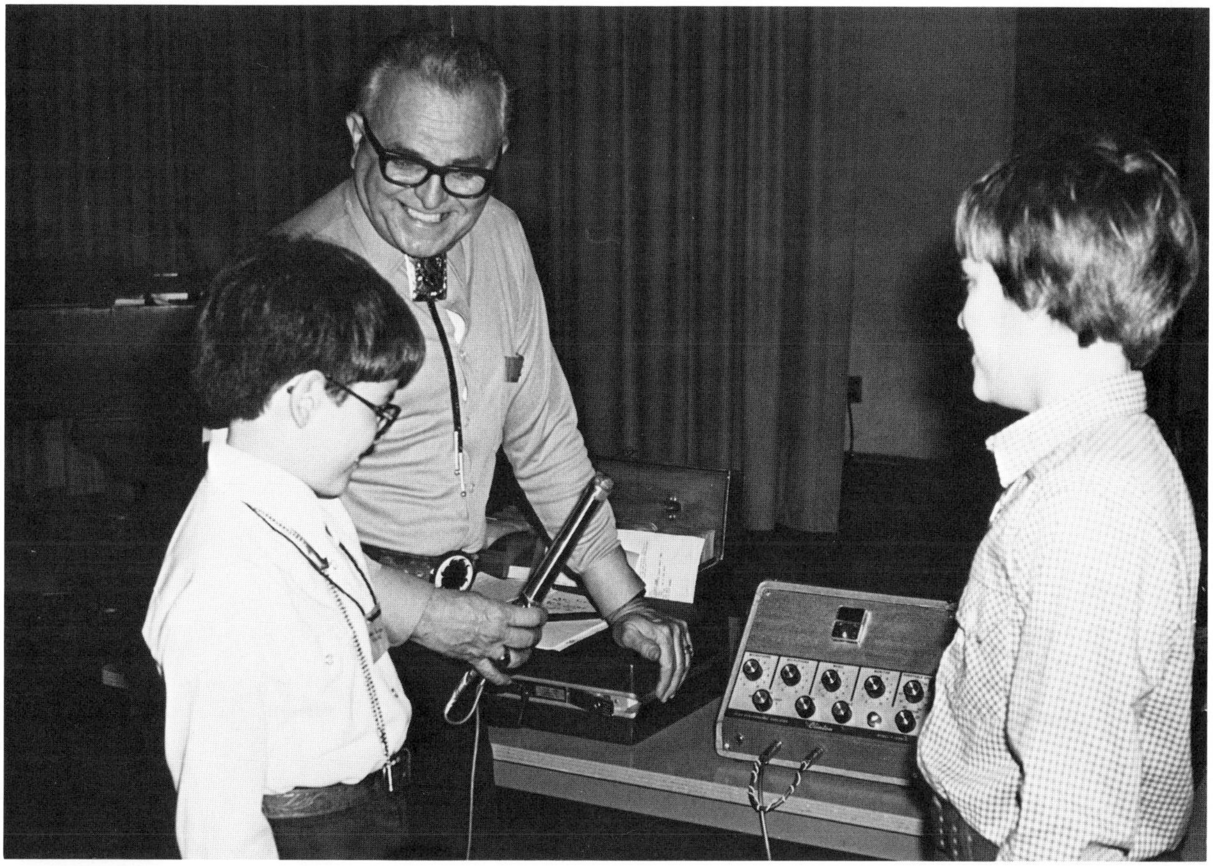

I remember one special invitation to a local adult square dance. Andrew and I learned many new things at this dance.

Andrew was interested in the equipment the live caller used, especially the microphone. The caller used the microphone to make his voice heard above the music. The caller did **singing calls** and **patter calls.** A singing call has words to fit a popular melody. The caller gives square dance instructions in place of some of the song's original words.

Patter calls are the kind that usually come to mind when you think of square dancing. The caller combines many calls into new patterns, and he gives these instructions while background music is playing. The music that goes with patter calls is called **hoedown music.** It has good rhythm for dancing.

At first it was strange dancing to a live caller. He had a list of calls we knew, but we were not used to hearing them in his patterns. We really had to concentrate. Some of the adult dancers helped us with the steps. One of our new adult friends is Frank. He is 80 years old and has been square dancing for 25 years.

Andrew and I have just started dancing. We know some basic calls, but we can't wait to learn more. Andrew and I hope that you will want to learn how to square dance, too. We think that square dancing is for everyone!

Words about SQUARE DANCING

ARCH: Partners' hands joined and raised above their heads

BREAK: To release hand holds

CALL: An instruction to do a particular square dance move. The calls described in this book are: *honor your partner; circle left and right; do-sa-do; see saw; promenade; courtesy turn; allemande left; right and left grand; weave the ring; right hand star; pass thru; California twirl; rollaway half sashay; grand square;* and *swing your partner.*

CLOCKWISE: In the direction the hands on a clock move

CURTSEY: A bowed greeting done by girls at the start of a dance

HEAD COUPLES: The dancers in positions 1 and 3 in the square

HOME POSITION: A dancer's starting position in the square

LIVE CALLER: A person who gives square dance calls

OPPOSITE: The dancer directly across from another at the beginning of a call

PATTER CALL: A series of calls given with background music

SIDE COUPLES: The dancers in positions 2 and 4 in the square

SINGING CALL: Square dance instructions given by the caller in place of a song's original words

SHUFFLE STEP: The toe-to-heel walking motion done in square dancing

SQUARE UP: To stand in the starting positions in the square

SQUARED SET: An imaginary square on the dance floor. Each pair of dancers stands on one side of the square.

TWIRL: A smooth dance movement in which the girl turns under the raised right arm of her partner

WORKSHOP: To learn new calls

About the Square Dancers in this Book

Michelle and Andrew's square dance group, the Mountain State Squares, is named for West Virginia, the state where they live. West Virginia's senator, Robert C. Byrd, introduced a special resolution to the United States Senate in Washington, D.C. His bill proposed to make square dancing the national folk dance of the United States.

Congressional Record
United States of America
PROCEEDINGS AND DEBATES OF THE 97th CONGRESS, FIRST SESSION
Vol. 127 WASHINGTON, MONDAY, MARCH 30, 1981 No. 51

DESIGNATION OF THE SQUARE DANCE AS THE NATIONAL FOLK DANCE OF THE UNITED STATES

Mr. ROBERT C. BYRD. Mr. President, today I am introducing a Senate joint resolution to signify the ebullient spirit of our society. I am calling for the designation of the square dance to be the national folk dance of the United States of America.

Our early settlers worked hard. When the week's work was done, they socialized. When they socialized, they danced. The Puritans danced, and so did the Cavaliers. These colonial caperers were no respecters of persons—high and low took their places in the "longways" and took their turns to swing and dip. George Washington, in the parlors of the 13 colonies, and Daniel Boone in the backwoods huts, understood the square dance, so-called from the adoption of the "squares" popularly danced in France. The square dance evolved in the ballrooms, log cabins, and wagon trains, and with the expansion of our Nation, spread from the mountains of the East to the prairies and the deserts of the West.

Built on a pyramid of folk dances, jigs, minuets, and contras, the square dance spread—ever changing, ever elaborating. Callers began to direct the dancers, their calls becoming familiar tunes—"swing your partner—right and left all around, sashay and promenade"—a strange mixture of French and English, and now Americana.

Every community has its own way of square dancing, and every fiddler his own way of playing the tunes. There is nothing like the square dance elsewhere in the world. Yet, the American square dance is popular today on the European continent, in Asia, in the Orient, Latin America, in every portion of the civilized world. Therefore, I feel this jolly envoy from our great Republic should be honored by my bill to designate the square dance to be the national folk dance of our country.

Mr. President, I ask unanimous consent that the joint resolution be printed in the RECORD.

There being no objection, the joint resolution was ordered to be printed in the RECORD, as follows:

S.J. RES. 59

Whereas square dancing has been a popular tradition in America since early colonial days;

Whereas square dancing has attained a revered status as part of the folklore of this country;

Whereas square dancing is a joyful expression of the vibrant spirit of the people of the United States;

Whereas the American people value the display of etiquette among men and women which is a major element of square dancing;

Whereas square dancing is a traditional form of family recreation which symbolizes a basic strength of this country, namely, the unity of the family;

Whereas square dancing epitomizes democracy because it dissolves arbitrary social distinctions; and

Whereas it is fitting that the square dance be added to the array of symbols of our national character and pride: Now, therefore, be it

Resolved by the Senate and House of Representatives of the United States of America in Congress assembled, That the square dance is designated the national folk dance of the United States of America.

The Mountain State Squares wanted to show their support of Senator Byrd's bill, so they planned a trip to Washington to meet Mr. Byrd and to dance for him.

When the Mountain State Squares arrived in Washington, they took a guided tour of the Capitol Building. There they met Mr. Byrd, and the senate photographer took pictures of the square dancers on the steps of the Capitol.

Senator Byrd was pleased when the dancers asked if they could dance for him. When they finished performing, the senator gave each dancer a packet of information about the Capitol, and he gave Ms. Sharp a copy of the resolution on square dancing. Later that year, President Ronald Reagan signed the bill, and square dancing officially became the national dance of the United States.

ABOUT THE AUTHOR

MILDRED HAMMOND and her husband, Forrest, teach square dance classes to adults and children. They have been members of several square dancing committees and clubs, including the Washington Area Square Dancers Cooperative Association, the West Virginia Square and Round Dance Organization, the Dancin' Nomads, the Blue Ridge Twirlers, The Westernaires, and the Grand Squares. Mrs. Hammond holds a master's degree in library science and is currently a children's librarian.

ABOUT THE PHOTOGRAPHER

JAMES C. TABB graduated from West Virginia University and then served as a captain in the U.S. Army. After returning from Europe, Tabb resumed studies at West Virginia University and received his master's degree. He has been a freelance photographer for 25 years.